Get Active at the Beach

by Sascha Goddard

OXFORD
UNIVERSITY PRESS
AUSTRALIA & NEW ZEALAND

Let's Get Active!

Have you been lucky enough to spend time at the beach?

Beaches are not only fun, they are also great places to get active. The sand and ocean offer many options for sport and other physical activities.

Let's take a look at some now!

People of all ages enjoy beach activities.

Sport on the Sand

Frisbee

A frisbee is a flat, round object designed to be thrown through the air. At the beach, you can throw a frisbee in any direction.

Throwing, catching and running after a frisbee are fun ways to be active.

Beach cricket

Beach cricket is a great sport for the whole family. There are fewer rules than in regular cricket.

To play, you need a cricket bat, a tennis ball and two sets of stumps or markers.

You can draw a line in the sand as a marker if you don't have stumps.

Someone **bowls** the ball to the batter. The aim is to hit the ball with the bat, then run between the stumps as many times as you can.

Other players try to catch the ball, or touch the stumps with it while you run.

When the ball touches the stumps, the batter is out.

Beach safety

Look around while playing and if people are walking past, wait. You don't want the ball to hit anyone.

Beach volleyball

Volleyball is played on a court, but did you know that it's played on the beach, too?

Volleyball players hit the ball upwards and over the net with their hands.

The sand makes a good court as players can dive down safely to get the ball.

Hitting the ball downwards over the net is called a spike.

Beach volleyball has been an official Olympic sport since 1996. **Professional** beach volleyball athletes are highly skilled at the game.

Amazing beach achievements

American athlete Kerri Walsh Jennings won 22 Olympic beach volleyball games in a row! She has three Olympic gold medals.

Beach Activities

Sand sculpting

Have you ever built a sandcastle? Wet sand is **ideal** for building.

Sand **sculpting** is a popular beach activity that anyone can enjoy, from young children to adults.

Decorate your sculpture with shells, sticks or seaweed!

Beach safety

Always be sun-smart at the beach. Protect your skin with sunscreen, a hat and clothes that cover you.

Sand sculpting is fun, but it can also be serious. Some people spend years learning how to build detailed sculptures. They use small spades, spatulas and even dentist tools!

Sand sculpting competitions are held all around the world.

Amazing beach achievements

A sculptor called Mark Anderson made the first ever sandcastle hotel. People could stay overnight.

Run or walk

Going for a walk or run at the beach is a simple, free way to keep fit.

Walking or running along the hard, wet sand beside the ocean is best. In the dry sand, your feet sink!

Bring your dog

Some dogs love having adventures at the beach. All the new sights and smells are exciting!

Dogs enjoy swimming, digging and chasing balls.

Playing fetch is good exercise for a dog and its owner.

Beach safety

Always check signs to see if dogs are allowed on the beach. And remember to pick up after your dog.

Rock pooling

At the beach, small pools of warm water form between rocks. These rock pools contain many tiny sea creatures.

Exploring rock pools is a fascinating activity. You might spot crabs or sea stars.

People sometimes use a bucket or net to get a closer look.

Beach safety

Don't touch sea creatures. They could hurt you, or you could easily hurt them.

Climbing over rocks, crouching down and stretching to look for creatures will keep your body flexible.

In the Water

Swimming

Ocean swimming gets your whole body moving.

Some people like to swim a long way, while others enjoy splashing in the **shallows**.

Ocean swimming is a fun way to cool off on a warm day.

Swimming in the ocean can be peaceful or exciting.

Sometimes you can float gently on the calm ocean. Or you can try to jump over **breaking** waves, or swim towards the shore, letting the waves push you in.

Beach safety

Always swim with someone else and stay between the flags. Lifeguards put the flags where it's safest to swim.

Bodyboarding

Bodyboarding is another way to catch a wave into the shore.

You lie on your front and wait for a wave, then paddle your arms and kick your legs. Sometimes the wave carries you right up onto the sand.

These bodyboarders stopped paddling and ride the wave.

Surfing

In surfing, the aim is to stand up on a surfboard and ride waves.

You need strength in your upper body and legs to be able to surf well. Practising surfing helps to build up your muscles.

Using your arms can help you balance.

Amazing beach achievements

Kelly Slater is one of the greatest surfers of all time. He won 11 world championships over almost 20 years!

Stand-up paddleboarding

Stand-up paddleboarding is another popular beach activity. The paddleboarder stands on top of a long, narrow board as it floats on the ocean. A long paddle is used to push the board through the water.

Two or three people can fit on a stand-up paddleboard at once.

It's best to first try paddleboarding on calm, flat water. But with further practice, you can ride rough waves, race and even do yoga on your board!

Keeping Beaches Clean

Beach pollution

Pollution on our beaches is a big issue. Lots of litter ends up in our water system and washes up on beaches.

Top 5 items polluting our beaches

1 Cigarette butts

2 Food wrappers

3 Straws and stirrers

4 Plastic drink bottles

5 Plastic bags

Cleaning up

Sometimes people have special beach clean-up days to pick up litter at local beaches.

We can all help so that everyone can continue to enjoy the beach.

These people are removing plastic from a polluted beach.

Fun at the Beach

Next time you visit the beach, think about what activities you could try.

Maybe you want to build a sand sculpture or learn how to surf. Perhaps you will explore a rock pool, then play some beach cricket.

Whatever you choose to do, stay safe, don't leave rubbish behind and, most of all, enjoy the beach!

Glossary

bowls: throws a ball to the person batting in cricket

breaking: waves rolling over and crashing down

ideal: perfect for something

professional: an expert who might get paid or win prizes for what they do

sculpting: shaping something with your hands

shallows: part of the ocean that is not very deep

Index